Ar   arent
Blac   ioney
they   ated"
matl   ed in
her   doc-
torat   or of
Rese

Scientist
and Administrator,
Antoinette Rodez
Schiesler

by Mary Ellen Verheyden-Hilliard

drawings by Marian Menzel

The Equity Institute

Bethesda, Maryland

This work was developed under a grant from the Women's Educational Equity Act Program, U.S. Department of Education. However, the content does not necessarily reflect the position of that Agency and no official endorsement of these materials should be inferred.

Library of Congress Cataloging in Publication Data

Verheyden-Hilliard, Mary Ellen.
  Scientist and administrator, Antoinette Rodez Schiesler.

  (An American women in science biography)
  Summary: Relates the story of an Afro-American woman who overcame childhood difficulties with mathematics and went on to earn a Ph.D. in chemistry.

  1. Schiesler, Antoinette Rodez—Juvenile literature. 2. Chemists—United States—Biography—Juvenile literature. [1. Schiesler, Antoinette Rodez. 2. Chemists. 3. Afro-Americans—Biography] I. Menzel, Marian, ill. II. Title. III. Series: Verheyden-Hilliard, Mary Ellen. American women in science biography.
QD22.S34V47   1985   540'.92'4 [B] [92]   84-25978
ISBN 0-932469-08-6

Scientist
and Administrator,
Antoinette Rodez
Schiesler

The steam from the heavy iron made a hissing sound on the wet white shirt. Twelve-year-old Toni Rodez stopped ironing and wiped her face. Ironing was hard work.

"How are you doing, Toni?" her mother asked.

"I'm okay, Mom." Toni often came after school to be with her mother at the laundry and dry cleaning store. Toni knew it was hard for many Black women to get jobs. Her mother said this job paid better than some.

After work, Toni and her mother walked to their apartment. They lived in a housing project in New Haven, Connecticut.

"I think I'll be able to finish your dress tonight," Toni's mother said as they walked along. There was little money for new clothes. Toni's mother fixed Toni's old dresses so they looked almost new. "Do you have much homework?"

"Just the same old, awful math," Toni said. Toni liked to read. She liked science class. But she hated math.

That night, Toni frowned as she read the math problems over and over. Finally she put her head in her hands. "I'll never understand it. I hate math! I quit!" The tears and the anger poured out. "Besides, I'll never have a chance. What's the use of working so hard?"

"And what if things change, Toni?" her mother said. "What if you do get a chance? And then you have to say you're not ready?"

"I know," Toni said. "But it's so hard. It's so hard every day."

"Excuses never get anything done, Toni," her mother said kindly.

Toni's mother thought a moment. "You know, Toni, maybe doing math is like training to be a track champion. Every single day she's out there running. Rain or snow. Every day she learns to run a little better. Training never ends if you want to be a champion."

"What kind of champion will I be, Mom?"

Toni's mother smiled. "Well, that's for you to decide. But I don't suppose you want to iron wet shirts forever."

Toni began to smile. The thought of ironing wet shirts forever made math seem easy. She picked up her pencil and started to work.

"Keep at it, Toni. I know you can do it," her mother said.

Antoinette Rodez was born on December 13, 1934. Her friends call her Toni. As she grew up, her mother encouraged her to learn about art and music. Toni and her mother often visited museums together. In the summer they went to free symphony concerts. The orchestra and the audience sat outside.

Toni loved the summer concerts. She and her mother went to almost every one.

Toni knew her mother wished she could give Toni everything she wanted. But there just wasn't enough money. Toni remembered the time she wanted an electric train. Her mother gave her a doll.

When Toni picked the doll up, it said "Mama!" Toni wanted to know what made the doll talk. She took it to her room and took the doll's head off. She found something inside that looked like a small drum. She pulled it out. She poked at it. "Mama!" it said. It was the doll's voice box.

Toni put the head back on the doll. She put the doll back in the box, but she took the voice box to school. It was more fun to play with than the doll!

Toni liked to build things as well as take them apart. She got different size boxes from the grocery store. She pasted the boxes together. Each box was a room in a little house. She cut holes in the sides for doors and windows.

Toni found old newspapers and magazines. She cut out pictures of tables and chairs, beds and lamps, rugs and curtains, even a bathtub and a stove. Then she pasted the pictures in the boxes. Toni had built herself a real doll house!

Toni's mother wanted Toni to have a better education. She borrowed money to send Toni to a boarding school. The teachers there were nuns. Toni studied hard. She still did not like math. But she found that learning math *was* like being in training. The more she worked at it, the easier it was to do.

After a year, the money Toni's mother had borrowed was used up. But Toni was such a good student, she was given a scholarship. She could go to the school free.

At school, Toni taught herself
to play the guitar. Her guitar
helped her make friends. Girls
always came to listen to Toni
play and to sing songs with her.

Toni got an "A" in every class. Even math! She was valedictorian for her class. That meant she had the best grades, and she gave the farewell speech at graduation.

When she was 17 years old, Toni decided to become a nun. The group of nuns she joined were teachers. After she became a nun, she went to college. Then she taught school for 11 years. Sometimes her students said that math was too hard. Toni just laughed. "No excuses," she always said. "I did it, and so can you!"

After years of teaching, Toni went back to college again to earn a doctorate in chemistry at the University of Maryland. A doctorate is the highest degree a scientist can earn.

Chemistry is the science that finds out what things are made of and how they can change. To study chemistry, Toni had to do many hard math problems. But she did not make excuses. She just did what she had to do.

Toni became an Academic Dean. She was in charge of helping teachers and students do the best they could in college.

After more than 20 years, Toni decided she should not be a nun any longer. She had loved her life

as a nun, but now she felt she
must begin a new life.

Toni went to work at the University of Maryland in the School of Pharmacy. There, students learned to be pharmacists. They learned about the chemistry of the medicines people take.

Toni wrote to her mother about her new job. "I am trying to get more Black students interested in becoming pharmacists," she wrote. "I hold meetings to tell students about pharmacy. Some of the workbooks the students use are not very good. So I have to write new math and science problems for the books. The little girl who had a hard time doing math problems is now writing problems for college students!"

Her mother wrote back, "I always said you could do it!"

After several years, Toni moved to Michigan. She became the Director of the Office of Research and Development at Eastern Michigan University. She married Robert Schiesler.

Toni helped people at the university find ways to pay for the research they want to do. Because she knows so much about math and science, she is able to help people write their research ideas clearly.

Toni is very interested in computers. "Computers are only a little harder to understand than my doll's voice box," she says with a smile.

"I want to get girls and boys interested in computers. A girl who knows how to make her doll talk should be learning how to make computers talk too."

In 1985 Toni moved to Pennsylvania. She became Director of Research at Villanova University.

Toni is often asked to talk with girls and boys about what they want to be. Sometimes she shares with them what she learned when she was a little girl.

"Be sure to take math no matter what you think you want to be. It helps you learn how to keep things organized. It helps you think more clearly.

"Math can be hard, but, believe me, it's worth the struggle.

"Just remember," Dr. Toni Rodez Schiesler says with a smile, "no excuses, you can do it!"